Safety First

Adria F. Klein

Publisher: Christine Yuen
Series Editors: Adria F. Klein & Alan Trussell-Cullen
Editors: Bob Rowland & Paige Sanderson
Photographer: Lois Stanfield
Designers: Gary Hamada & Lois Stanfield

Copyright ©2001 Dominie Press, Inc. All rights reserved. No part of this publication may be reproduced or transmitted in any form or by any means without permission in writing from the publisher. Reproduction of any part of this book, through photocopy, recording, or any electronic or mechanical retrieval system, without the written permission of the publisher, is an infringement of the copyright law.

Published by:

Dominie Press, Inc.

1949 Kellogg Avenue
Carlsbad, California 92008 USA

www.dominie.com

ISBN 0-7685-0582-8

Printed in Singapore by PH Productions Pte Ltd

3 4 5 6 PH 03

Table of Contents

Safe on My Bike	4
Safe on My Skateboard	6
Safe in the Car	8
Safe on Roller Skates	10
Safety First	16
Picture Glossary	20
Index	20

I like to ride my bike.
I wear a helmet for safety.
I do not want to get hurt.

6

I like to ride on my skateboard.
I wear a helmet and kneepads for safety.

8

I like to ride in the car with my mom.
Mom and I wear seat belts for safety.
It is important to be safe.

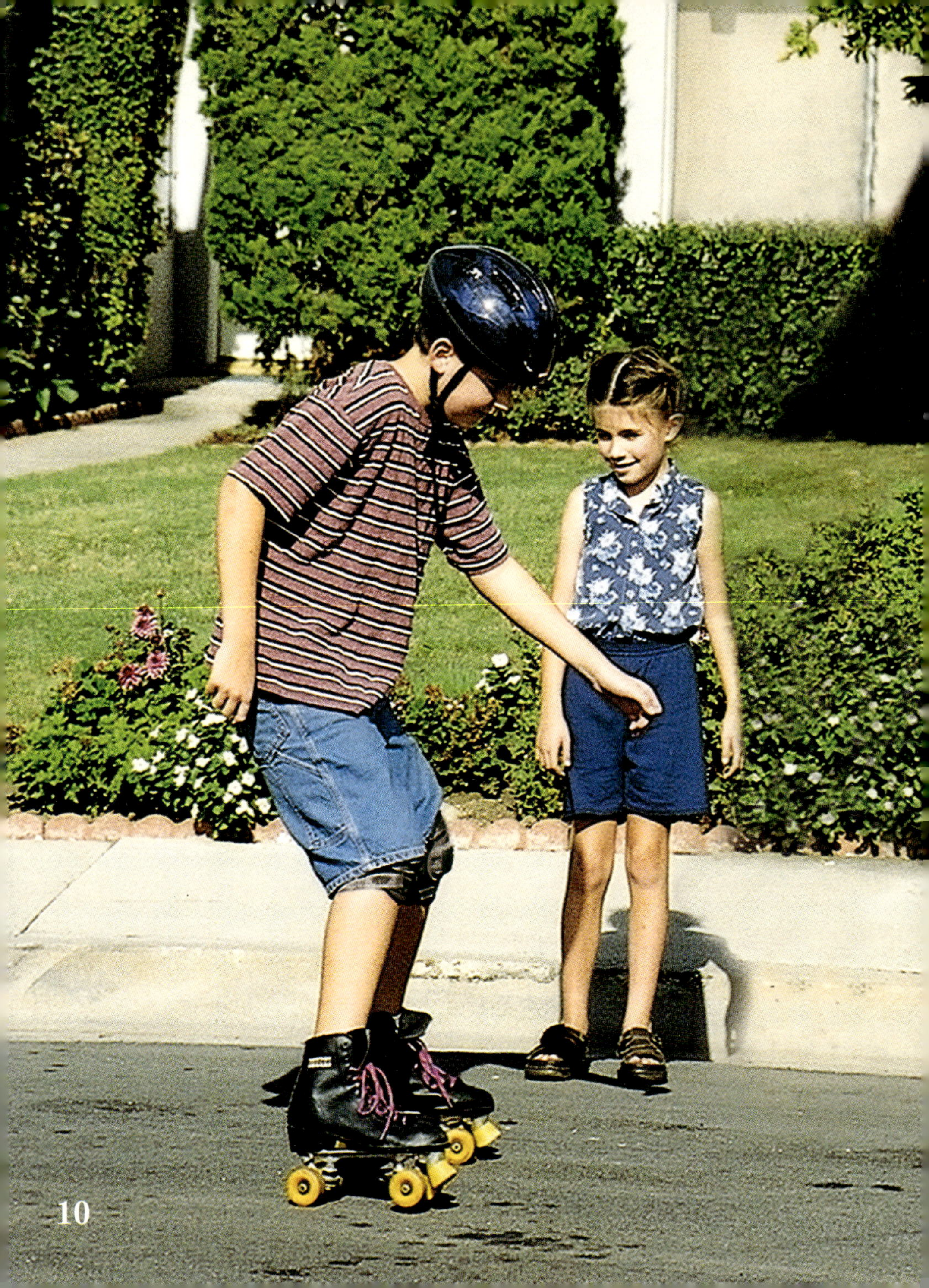

I want to learn how to roller-skate.
My brother is going to teach me how to roller-skate.
Mom says I have to be safe.

12

We go to the store to buy skates.

Mom and I talk with the man at the store.

He tells me how to be safe when I roller-skate.

CHILD
YOUTH
ADULT
RECOMMENDED AGE 14 & UP
AGGRESSIVE SKATE HELMET
$12.99

I need a helmet.
I can use the same helmet
I use when I ride my bicycle.

I need some kneepads.
I can use the same kneepads
I use when I ride
on my skateboard.

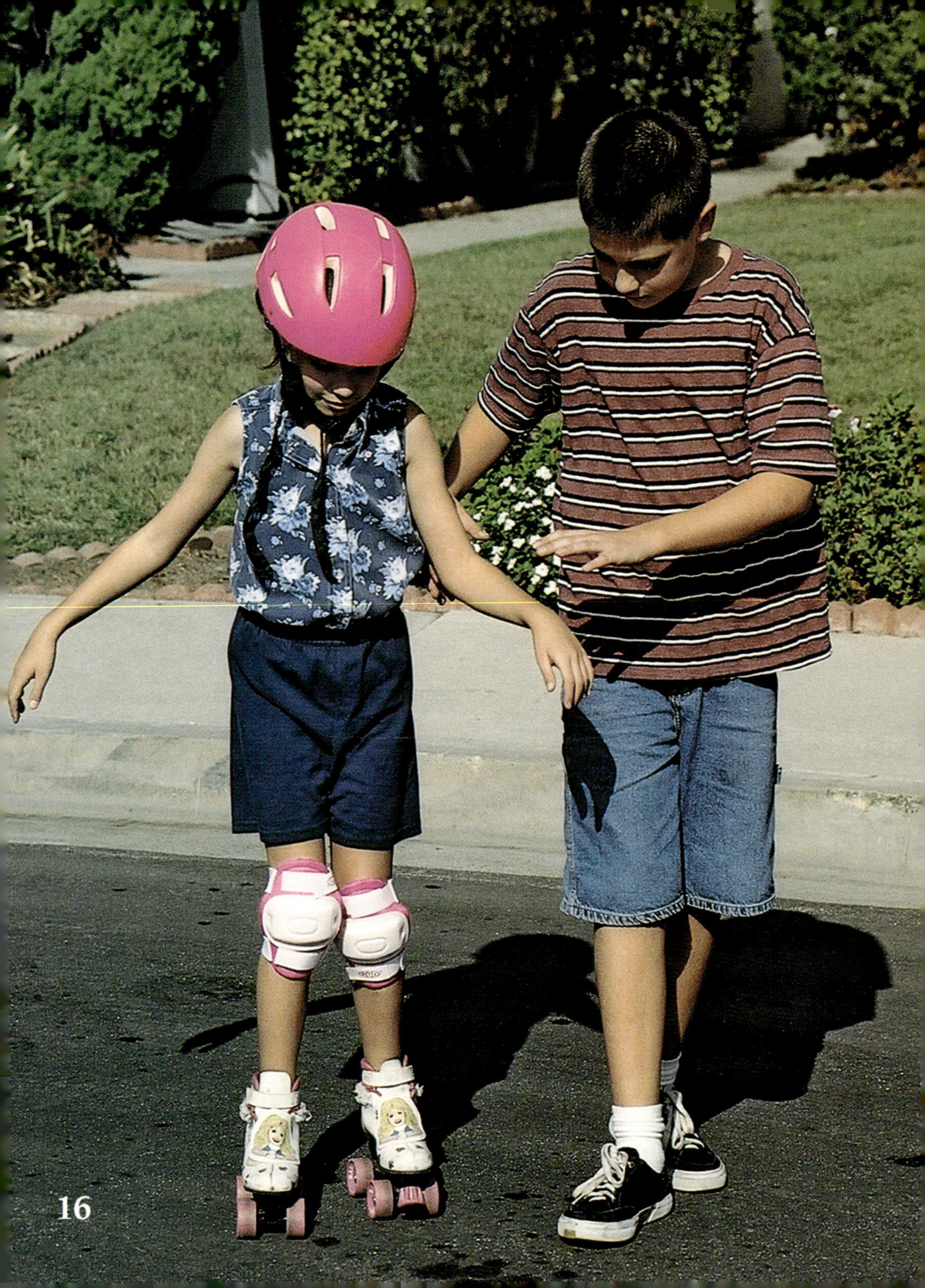

I am all ready to learn how
to roller-skate.
My brother gives me
my first lesson.
I want to be safe.
I have my helmet.
I have my kneepads.
I try my best, but . . .

18

... I keep falling down! Maybe I need a pillow for my seat!

Picture Glossary

helmet:

skateboard:

kneepads:

skates:

Index

bike, 5
car, 9
helmet, 5, 7, 15, 17
kneepads, 7, 15, 17
pillow, 19

roller-skate, 11, 13, 17
seat belts, 9
skateboard, 7, 15
skates, 13
store, 13